AF270403

PAWESOME DOG AWARDS

Written by Annabel Griffin

Illustrated by Marina Halak

Copyright © 2024 Hungry Tomato Ltd

First published in 2024 by Hungry Tomato Ltd
F15, Old Bakery Studios, Blewetts Wharf, Malpas Road, Truro, Cornwall,
TR1 1QH, UK.

A CIP catalog record for this book is available from the British Library.

ISBN 9781916598089

Manufactured in the USA

Discover more at
www.hungrytomato.com

CONTENTS

Words in **BOLD** can be found in the glossary.

THE WORLD OF DOGS

Get ready to explore the wonderful world of pawesome dogs! From the hairiest dogs to the longest, there are so many different types of lovable dogs to discover.

WHERE DO DOGS COME FROM?

Believe it or not, all dogs are **descendants** of ancient wolves. The details of how and when wolves became dogs are still quite foggy, but it likely started when humans began to **domesticate** and train wolves, at least 14,000 years ago. Today, dogs can be found all over the world.

WHAT IS A BREED?

A breed is a particular group of dogs that all share the same (or very similar) appearance and **characteristics**, making them easy to identify. There are hundreds of different breeds, and they can vary wildly in size, shape, hairiness, and personality.

Not all dogs belong to a specific breed. Some dogs, known as mutts or mongrels, are a mixture of lots of different breeds. They can make fantastic pets, and can often be found looking for a loving home at rescue or **rehoming shelters.**

GETTING A DOG?

Maybe you already have a dog in your family, or maybe you'd like to in the future. Owning a dog can be fun and rewarding, but it's also a big responsibility. Some dogs need a lot of space, time and attention. Before buying or **adopting** a dog, you should always carefully research their breed and think about whether you are able to give them everything they need to be happy.

BREED GROUPS

Dog breeds are often arranged into seven different groups, that are loosely based on the jobs that they were originally bred to do.

SPORTING GROUP

Also known as gundogs, these dogs were originally bred to help hunters retrieve birds.

NON-SPORTING GROUP

This is the group for dogs that don't fit into any of the other groups, so they are quite a mixed bunch!

TERRIER GROUP

This group were originally bred to hunt burrowing animals, such as rats, rabbits, foxes, and badgers. Most of them have "terrier" as part of their name.

WORKING GROUP

Dogs in this group were originally bred to perform practical tasks, such as pulling sleds and carts. They were also often used as watchdogs. They are usually large dogs.

HOUND GROUP

Hounds were bred for their sense of smell or sight, and were usually used for hunting. They can be split into two sub-groups: sighthounds and scent hounds.

HERDING GROUP

This group includes dogs that were bred to work on farms; herding and guarding livestock, such as sheep and cows.

TOY GROUP

Tiny breeds that are small enough to sit in your lap fall into this group. They are bred mostly as pets and companions.

PAWESOME DOG AWARDS

Welcome to the Pawesome Dog Awards! We're celebrating dogs who dare to be different. From the biggest to the smallest, the fluffiest to the spottiest, these dogs all have something that makes them stand out from the crowd. Dotty dalmatians, popular poodles, and the rare yodelling New Guinea singing dog, all feature on the list of amazing award winners. Which dog would you give the award for funniest hairdo?

Irish Wolfhound

The award for the tallest dog goes to the Irish wolfhound. This shaggy dog can reach a whopping 34 inches (86cm) in height and weighs up to 150 pounds (68kg). They are gentle giants who love spending time with their humans.

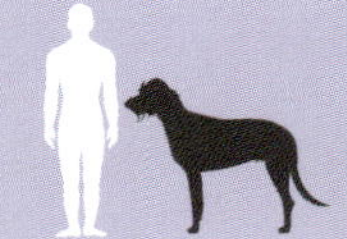

ORIGIN: Ireland

COAT: Medium-length, **wiry**

PERSONALITY: Patient and easy-going

INTELLIGENCE

ENERGY LEVEL

TRAINABILITY

Chihuahua

The Chihuahua is the smallest dog in the world, weighing no more than 6 pounds (3kg) and as little as 5 inches (13cm) tall. These dogs have a BIG PERSONALITY in a pocket-size body!

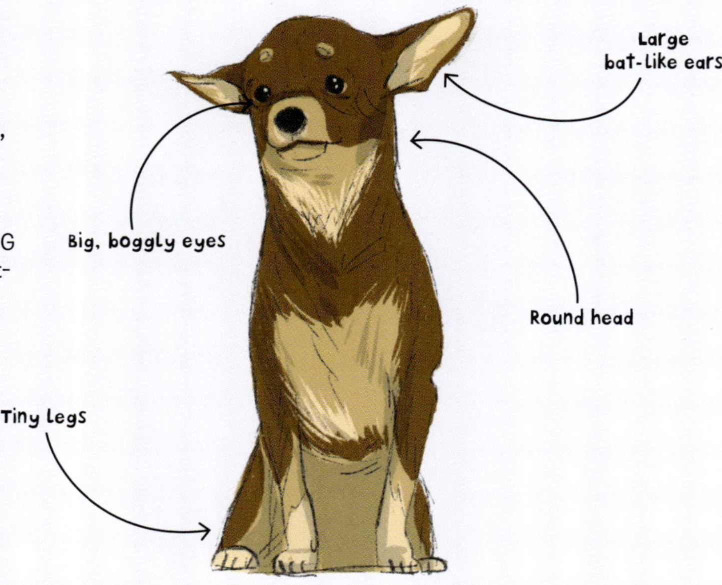

ORIGIN: Mexico

COAT: Short or medium-length, smooth

PERSONALITY: Alert and sassy

INTELLIGENCE

ENERGY LEVEL

TRAINABILITY

Bulldog

Bulldogs are well known for their short, upturned noses. This famous breed are known for being brave and friendly, but they can also be quite stubborn.

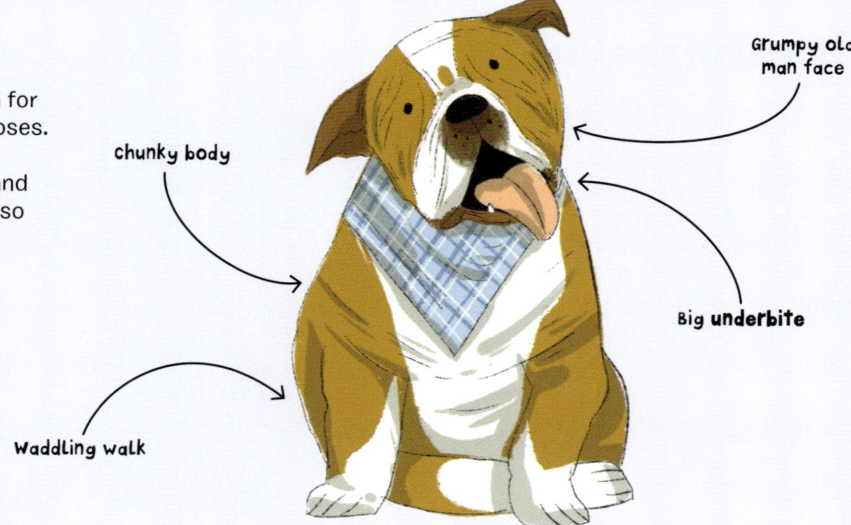

ORIGIN: United Kingdom

COAT: Short, smooth

PERSONALITY: Sweet and goofy

INTELLIGENCE

ENERGY LEVEL

TRAINABILITY

Affenpinscher

Affenpinschers have monkey-like looks, with a flat face and tiny nose with wide nostrils. These little dogs are confident, curious and funny.

ORIGIN: Germany

COAT: Medium-length, wiry

PERSONALITY: Mischievous and stubborn

INTELLIGENCE

ENERGY LEVEL

TRAINABILITY

Bull Terrier

Bull terriers are famous for their long "egg heads", and sloping noses. They are playful and clownish characters with bundles of confidence.

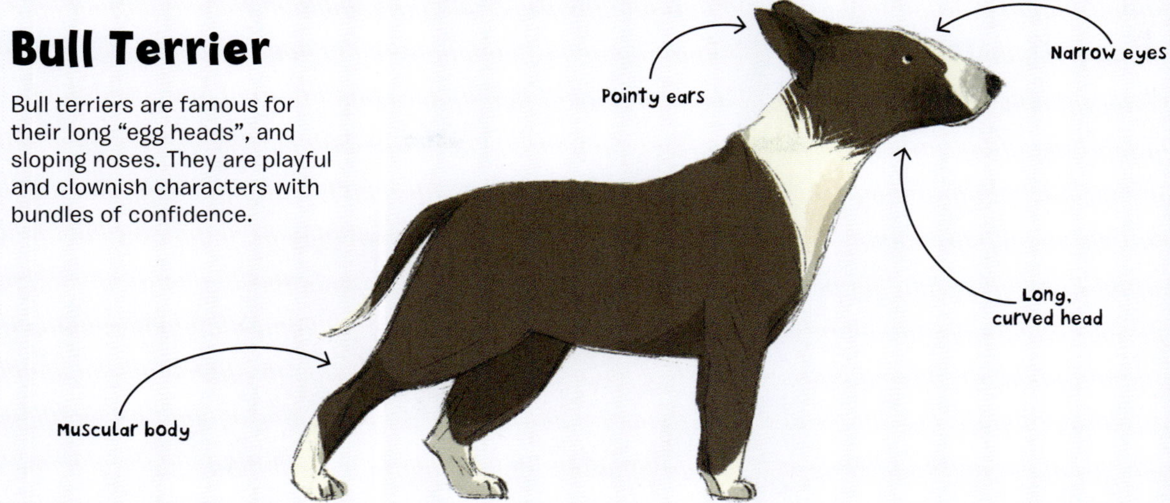

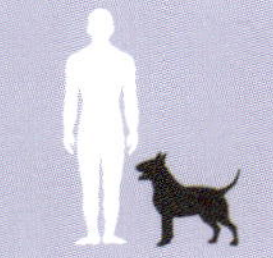

ORIGIN: United Kingdom

COAT: Short, smooth

PERSONALITY: Fun and feisty

INTELLIGENCE 

ENERGY LEVEL 

TRAINABILITY  

Borzoi

The winner of the longest nose award has to go to the borzoi. Their proud, regal look matches their history, as they were originally bred to hunt wolves for Russian **tsars** and nobles.

ORIGIN: Russia

COAT: Medium-length, wavy, silky

PERSONALITY: Calm and graceful

INTELLIGENCE 

ENERGY LEVEL 

TRAINABILITY   

Dachshund

Affectionately known as "sausage dogs", dachshunds are famous for their long bodies and little legs. They are a much-loved breed with a big personality. They are alert and loud, and make good little watchdogs.

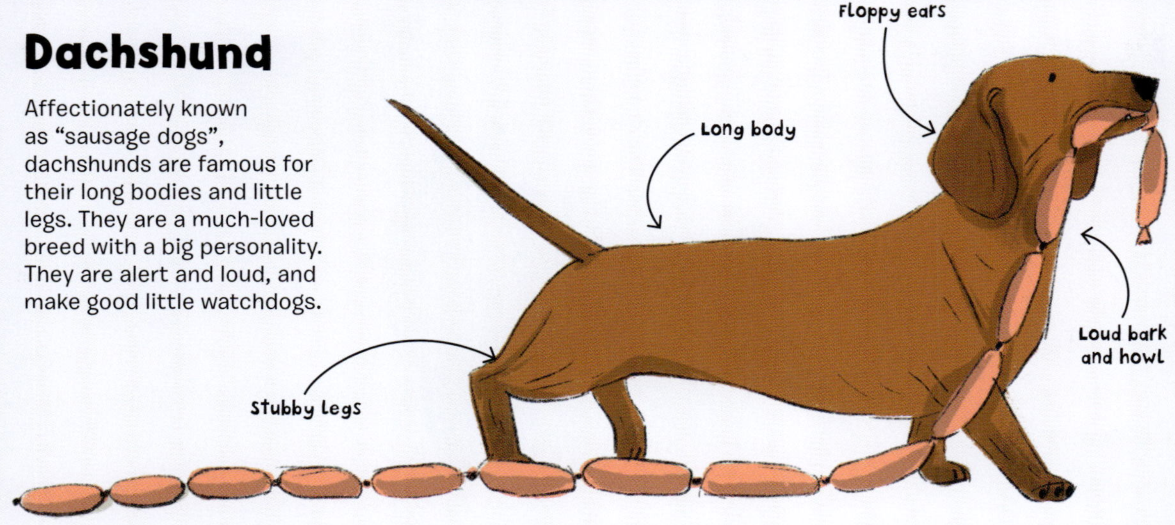

ORIGIN: Germany

COAT: Short, smooth/short, wiry/long, silky

PERSONALITY: Lovable but stubborn

	INTELLIGENCE	ENERGY LEVEL	TRAINABILITY

Dandie Dinmont Terrier

These funny-looking little dogs have one of the lowest tummies around! They were bred to fit down badger **burrows**, which helps to explain their long and low shape!

ORIGIN: United Kingdom

COAT: Medium, thick

PERSONALITY: Charming and social

INTELLIGENCE

ENERGY LEVEL

TRAINABILITY

Skye Terrier

Skye terriers have a big body on little legs. They are very loyal, brave, and affectionate companions.

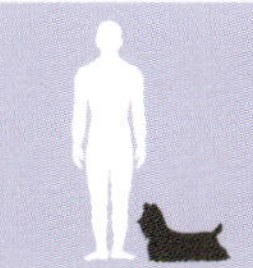

ORIGIN: United Kingdom

COAT: Long, silky

PERSONALITY: Loving and confident

INTELLIGENCE 

ENERGY LEVEL 

TRAINABILITY 

Bichon Frisé

These fluffy little dogs have a personality as cuddly as their looks. They require a lot of grooming to get them looking their best, puffiest self.

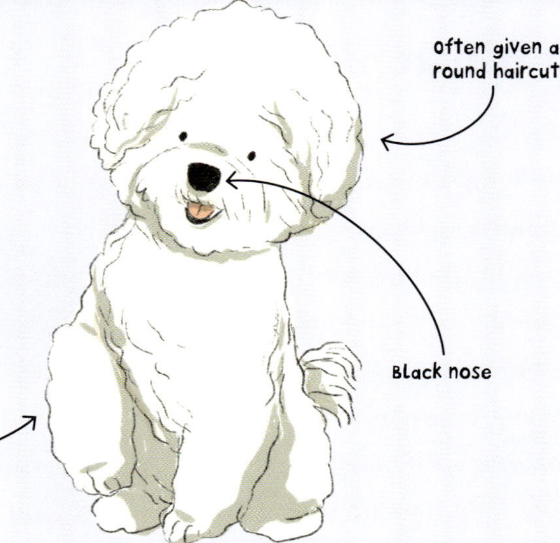

ORIGIN: The Canary Islands (Spain)

COAT: Medium-length, curly

PERSONALITY: Confident and affectionate

INTELLIGENCE	🐾 🐾 🐾 🐾 ⚪
ENERGY LEVEL	🐾 🐾 🐾 🐾 ⚪
TRAINABILITY	🐾 🐾 🐾 🐾 ⚪

Keeshond

These gorgeous fluffy dogs were first used as watch dogs on barge boats along the canals of the Netherlands. They are smart and easy to train.

ORIGIN: The Netherlands

COAT: Long, very thick

PERSONALITY: Friendly and inquisitive

INTELLIGENCE	🐾 🐾 🐾 🐾 🐾
ENERGY LEVEL	🐾 🐾 🐾 🐾 ⚪
TRAINABILITY	🐾 🐾 🐾 🐾 🐾

Pekingese

The Pekingese started off as a royal **lapdog** in China. It was only allowed to be owned by members of the Imperial Palace. They can be snooty with strangers, but are loving towards their owners.

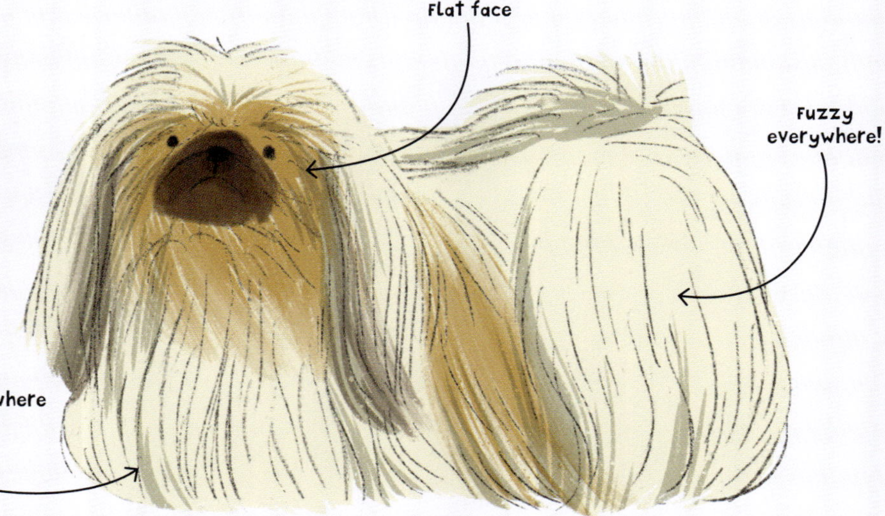

ORIGIN: China

COAT: Long, very thick

PERSONALITY: Charming and relaxed

INTELLIGENCE

ENERGY LEVEL

TRAINABILITY

Chow Chow

Despite their fluffy appearance, chow chows aren't known for being the friendliest dogs. Though they can form close bonds with their owners, they aren't big cuddlers. They are usually quiet and suspicious of strangers.

ORIGIN: China

COAT: Medium-length, very thick

PERSONALITY: Calm and independent

INTELLIGENCE

ENERGY LEVEL

TRAINABILITY

Afghan Hound

This glamorous, ancient sighthound has an extra-long, silky coat, which would have originally protected them from extreme weather conditions in the mountains of Afghanistan.

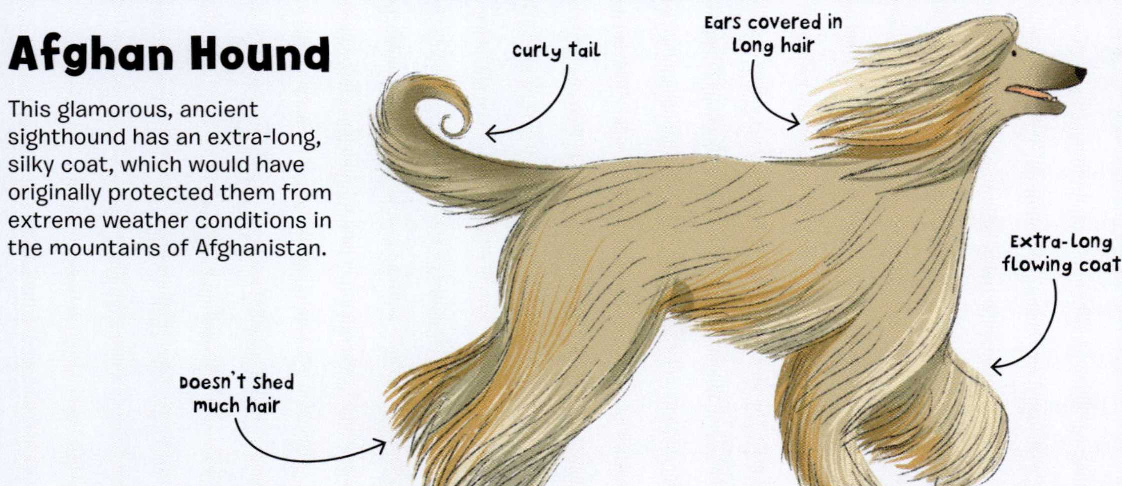

ORIGIN: Afghanistan

COAT: Long, silky

PERSONALITY: Independent and gentle

INTELLIGENCE

ENERGY LEVEL

TRAINABILITY

Komondor

These Hungarian sheepdogs have one of the longest and most unusual coats around. Covered from head to toe in long, tasselled cords, these dogs stand out!

ORIGIN: Hungary

COAT: Long, **corded**

PERSONALITY: Brave and affectionate

INTELLIGENCE

ENERGY LEVEL

TRAINABILITY

Yorkshire Terrier

You wouldn't think it from their beauty-pageant looks, but these little dogs were originally bred to catch rats in mills and mines of Northern England. They are elegant but scrappy little dogs, with big personalities.

ORIGIN: United Kingdom

COAT: Long, silky

PERSONALITY: Confident and friendly

INTELLIGENCE

ENERGY LEVEL

TRAINABILITY

Bearded Collie

The bearded collie's long, shaggy coat is perfect for working outdoors in all weather. These friendly, tireless, working sheepdogs can also make loving pets.

ORIGIN: United Kingdom

COAT: Long, silky, thick

PERSONALITY: Playful and affectionate

INTELLIGENCE

ENERGY LEVEL

TRAINABILITY

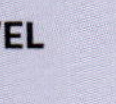

Bedlington Terrier

These fluffy terriers look like little lambs. Their traditional **"show clip"** gives them an unusual curved head shape. They are speedy, athletic and caring dogs, with a big bark.

ORIGIN: United Kingdom

COAT: Medium-length, curly

PERSONALITY: Cheerful and loyal

INTELLIGENCE

ENERGY LEVEL

TRAINABILITY

Chinese Crested

This dog's odd looks may not be everyone's cup of tea, but they make lively and affectionate lapdogs. They often need to wear a jumper to keep warm in the winter, and have to avoid the hot sun in the summer, as their skin burns easily.

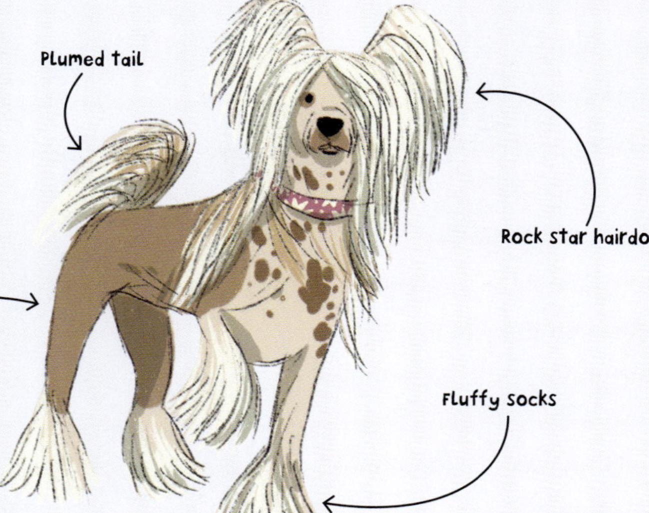

ORIGIN: China

COAT: Mostly hairless with long, silky areas

PERSONALITY: Friendly and social

INTELLIGENCE

ENERGY LEVEL

TRAINABILITY

Poodle

The dog best known for its fancy haircuts has to be the poodle! Many owners like to clip and groom their pet's fur into all kinds of different shapes. However, there is much more to poodles than their looks! They are one of the most intelligent dog breeds.

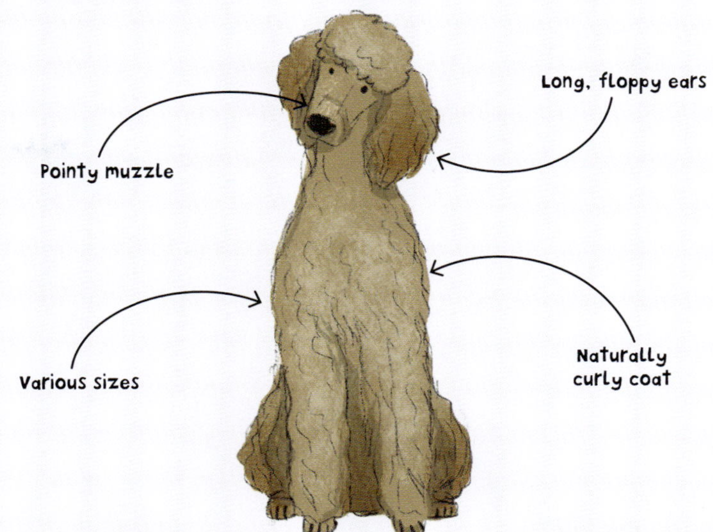

ORIGIN: Germany

COAT: Medium/long, curly/corded

PERSONALITY: Smart and active

INTELLIGENCE

ENERGY LEVEL

TRAINABILITY

Poodle Haircuts

Dalmatian

This dog is hard to miss, thanks to its iconic spotty coat. Each dalmatian's coat is unique, with a different pattern and number of spots. Puppies are born completely white, with their spots starting to show after a few weeks.

Dalmatians have a history of working as "coach dogs". They would trot alongside carriages to protect the people inside and their horses from robbers. Today, they make loyal family pets.

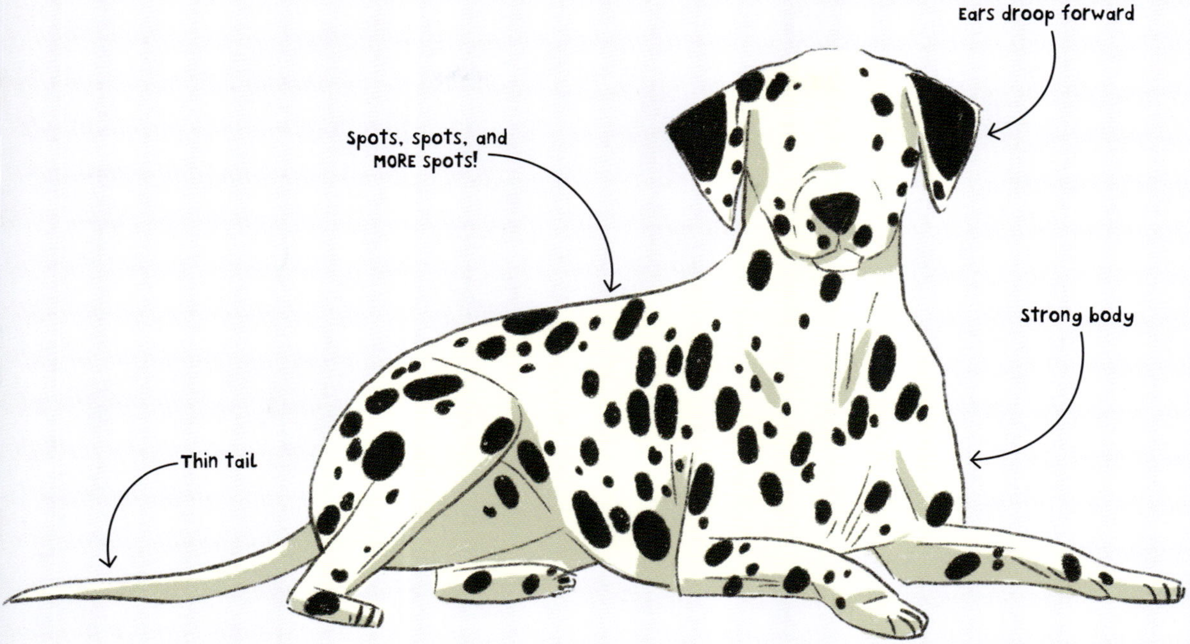

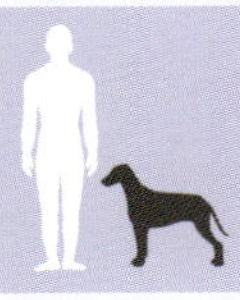

ORIGIN: Croatia

COAT: Short, smooth

PERSONALITY: Bright but shy

INTELLIGENCE

ENERGY LEVEL

TRAINABILITY

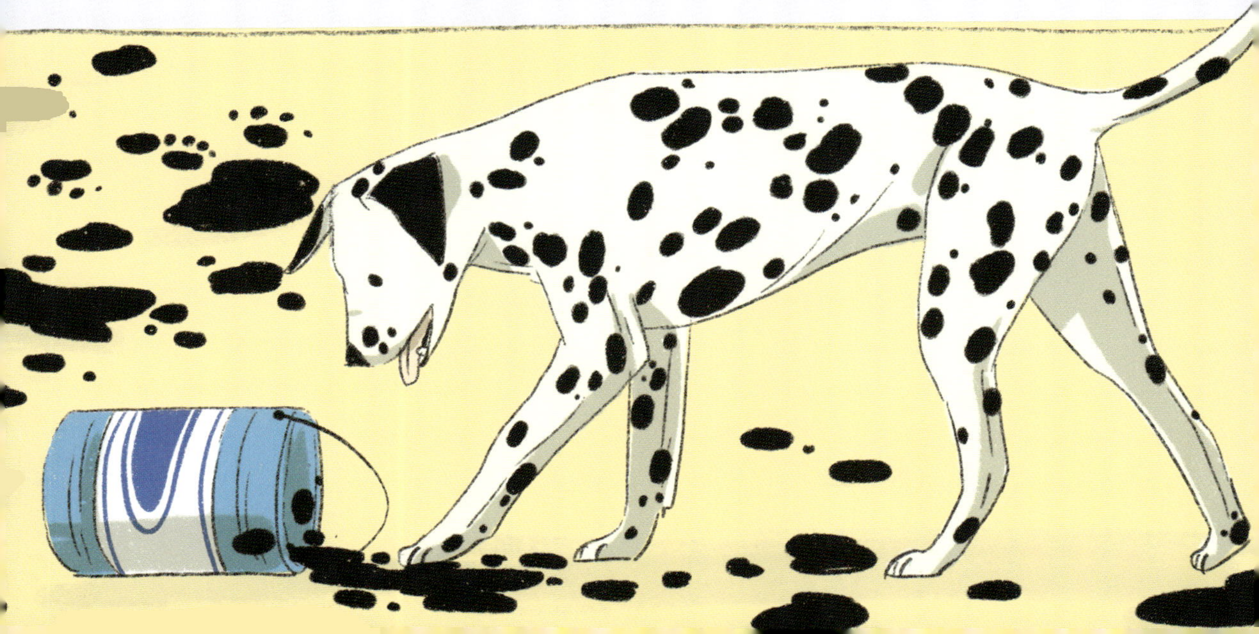

Pharaoh Hound

The pharaoh hound is actually a fairly modern breed, but it bears a very strong resemblance to dogs shown in artwork from ancient Egypt. They are elegant, graceful dogs that can make playful and loving pets.

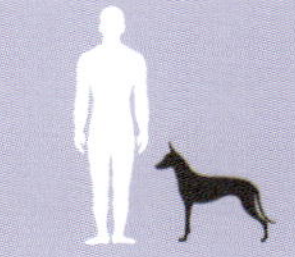

ORIGIN: Malta

COAT: Short, smooth

PERSONALITY: Sensitive and affectionate

INTELLIGENCE

ENERGY LEVEL

TRAINABILITY

Xoloitzcuintli (Mexican Hairless)

This unusual hairless breed is thought to date back at least 3,500 years! They were important to both ancient Maya and Aztec people, and it was believed that they could help to guide their dead owners into the afterlife.

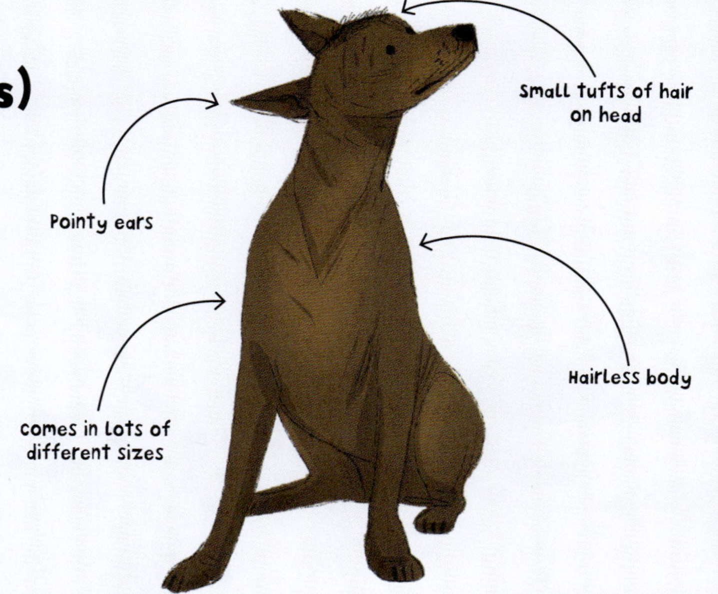

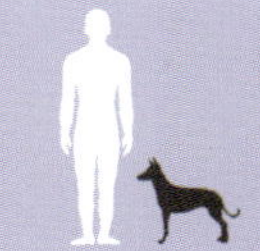

ORIGIN: Mexico

COAT: Hairless

PERSONALITY: Thoughtful and smart

INTELLIGENCE

ENERGY LEVEL

TRAINABILITY

New Guinea Singing Dog

This ancient breed is closely related to the Australian dingo. As their name suggests, they have a special talent for "singing". They have tuneful, yodel-like howls, and sometimes "sing" together, in a chorus. They mostly live semi-wild, so don't make easy pets.

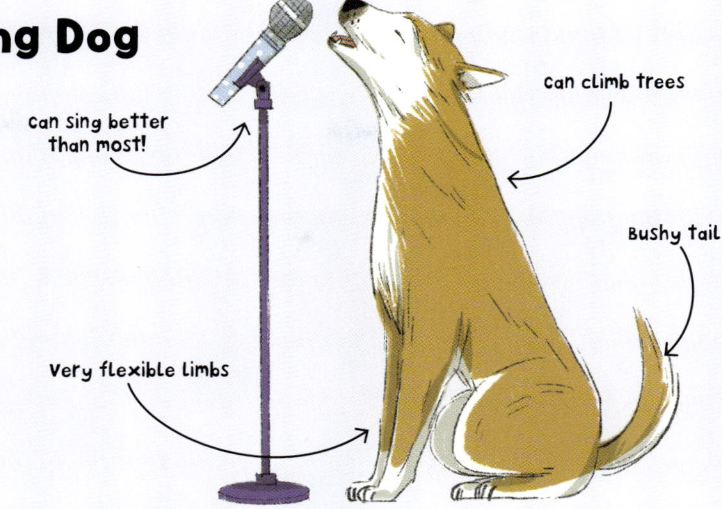

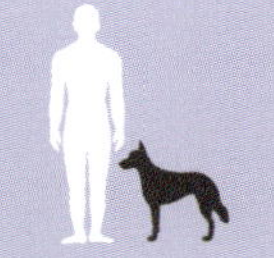

ORIGIN: New Guinea

COAT: Short, thick

PERSONALITY: Smart and Independent

INTELLIGENCE

ENERGY LEVEL

TRAINABILITY

Basenji

The basenji is an ancient breed of African hunting dog. It doesn't bark, but makes yodelling noises, similar to the New Guinea singing dog. Cave paintings of similar-looking dogs have been found in Libya that date back 6,000 years.

ORIGIN: Democratic Republic of the Congo

COAT: Short, smooth

PERSONALITY: Smart and Independent

INTELLIGENCE

ENERGY LEVEL

TRAINABILITY

WHAT'S THAT DOG?

Now that you have read all about these awesome dogs, how good are you at identifying them? There are 25 different dogs to figure out. Use the information in the book to help you.

What am I?
A. New Guinea
   Singing Dog
B. Chinese Crested
C. Komondor

What am I?
A. Pharaoh Hound
B. Bulldog
C. Bearded Collie

What am I?
A. Irish Wolfhound
B. Dachshund
C. Yorkshire Terrier

What am I?
A. Xoloitzcuintli
B. Dandie Dinmont Terrier
C. Poodle

What am I?
A. Bull Terrier
B. Bichon Frisé
C. Komondor

What am I?
A. Borzoi
B. Bulldog
C. Basenji

What am I?
A. Bearded Collie
B. Dachshund
C. Pharaoh Hound

What am I?
A. Dalmatian
B. New Guinea
   Singing Dog
C. Chinese Crested

What am I?
A. Bedlington Terrier
B. Bull Terrier
C. Bearded Collie

What am I?
A. Afghan Hound
B. Dandie Dinmont Terrier
C. Poodle

What am I?
A. Dalmatian
B. Dachshund
C. Skye Terrier

What am I?
A. Chihuahua
B. Pekingese
C. Komondor

What am I?

A. Keeshond
B. Chinese Crested
C. Bulldog

Answers can be found on page 32.

What am I?

A. Pekingese
B. Yorkshire Terrier
C. Skye Terrier

What am I?

A. Chihuahua
B. Bull Terrier
C. Pharaoh Hound

What am I?

A. Affenpinscher
B. Xoloitzcuintli
C. Poodle

What am I?

A. Keeshond
B. Irish Wolfhound
C. Affenpinscher

What am I?

A. Dachshund
B. Chinese Crested
C. Komondor

What am I?

A. Skye Terrier
B. Afghan Hound
C. Poodle

What am I?

A. Yorkshire Terrier
B. Bulldog
C. Bedlington Terrier

What am I?

A. Bichon Frisé
B. Irish Wolfhound
C. Xoloitzcuintli

What am I?

A. Borzoi
B. Dalmatian
C. Keeshond

What am I?

A. Chow Chow
B. Basenji
C. Borzoi

What am I?

A. Pekingese
B. Basenji
C. Pharaoh Hound

What am I?

A. Poodle
B. Chow Chow
C. Affenpinscher

SPOT THE DOG

There are so many brilliant dogs in the world. You can see them everywhere you go: in towns, parks, and sometimes even at the beach! See which of these are the most popular dogs where you live, make a note of them in a journal if you do spot them.

Chihuahua

Borzoi

Skye Terrier

Pekingese

Bearded Collie

Chow Chow

Dachshund

Bull Terrier

Affenpinscher

Poodle

Dalmatian

Bichon Frisé

TRAINING AND REWARDS

Trained dogs tend to be well behaved, easier to live with and easier to take out and about.

Training

Dogs are very clever, so you can train them to do lots of things. It's easier to teach dogs good habits when they are young. Correcting an older dog to behave is much harder.

You can also teach dogs tricks and commands. Their ability to follow commands is called **obedience**. The basic commands that most dogs are taught are:

Rewards

Rewarding your dog teaches them that they did something right. This is an important part of training.

You can reward your dog by giving them lots of fuss, attention and a tasty treat!

Agility

Agility is a sport where dogs complete an obstacle course as quickly and as accurately as possible. Obstacles include ramps, tunnels, and bars to jump over.

Trainers, called handlers, instruct their dog with voice cues and body signals – there are no toys or treats in sight!

Most owners start training their dogs at home, before taking them to agility classes, with other dogs to practice.

It takes a lot of training to win some of the top international competitions.

GLOSSARY

Adopting – Legally taking on the animal as your own, receiving all responsibility.

Agility (dog sport) – a sport where dogs complete complicated obstacle courses, including objects that they have run through, around, under, or jump over.

Burrows – holes or tunnels dug by animals.

Characteristics – a feature or quality of a person, place, or thing.

Corded – a type of dog coat that forms into long rope-like strands, similar to dreadlocks.

Descendants – people or animals that are related to an individual or group who lived in the past. For example, you are a descendant of your parents and grandparents.

Domesticate – to be tamed or trained to live or work with humans.

Lapdogs – dogs that are small enough to sit on someone's lap and make friendly companions.

Obedience – the ability to follow orders and commands. Obedience in dogs shows that training has been successful.

Rehoming shelter – a place where dogs (or other animals) who were lost, stray, or given up by their owners, are looked after until they can be adopted into a new home.

Show clip – a haircut or style used on dogs that compete in dog shows.

Tsar - a Russian emperor, before 1917.

Underbite (or undershot) – when the lower jaw or teeth stick out in front of the upper jaw or teeth, when the mouth is closed.

Wiry – a type of dog coat that is rough, thick, and bristly.

INDEX

WHAT'S THAT DOG ANSWERS

1 - B. Chinese Crested
2 - A. Pharaoh Hound
3 - A. Irish Wolfhound
4 - B. Dandie Dinmont Terrier
5 - C. Komondor
6 - B. Bulldog
7 - A. Bearded Collie
8 - B. New Guinea Singing Dog

9 - B. Bull Terrier
10 - A. Afghan Hound
11 - C. Skye Terrier
12 - B. Pekingese
13 - A. Keeshond
14 - B. Yorkshire Terrier
15 - A. Chihuahua
16 - B. Xoloitzcuintli
17 - C. Affenpinscher

18 - A. Dachshund
19 - C. Poodle
20 - C. Bedlington Terrier
21 - A. Bichon Frisé
22 - B. Dalmatian
23 - C. Borzoi
24 - B. Basenji
25 - B. Chow Chow

ABOUT THE AUTHOR

Annabel is a writer and artist based in London, UK. Having worked as a bookseller for many years, she now writes children's books focusing on animals and the natural world. Her recent titles include *What Can I See in the Wild?*, *Seasons* and *The Spectacular Lives of Sharks*.

ABOUT THE ILLUSTRATOR

Marina is a talented illustrator of children's books from Ukraine. Her stunning illustrations are inspired by her own childhood, children, nature, magical moments and fairytales.